MARSHALLPLAN

And

REVITALIZATION

Of The

UNITED STATES OF AMERICA

EUGENIO MACIAS

"Marshall Plan and Revitalization of the United States of America," by Eugenio Macias. ISBN 978-1-60264-259-1 (hard).

Published 2008 by Virtualbookworm.com Publishing Inc., P.O. Box 9949, College Station, TX 77842, US. ©2008, Eugenio Macias. All rights reserved. No part of this publication may be reproduced, stored in a retrieval system, or transmitted in any form or by any means, electronic, mechanical, recording or otherwise, without the prior written permission of Eugenio Macias.

Manufactured in the United States of America.

The future of America is in the hands of its people.
I dedicate this book to Our President and Congress.

FOREWORD

This book is my opinion, an assessment, of the past, present and future of the USA, and a guide as to what we can do to restore America's greatness and improve our quality of life. It is based on my life experience, conversations with people from all walks of life, books, magazines, newspaper articles and television news and documentaries.

America is abundant in opportunity and is a beautiful, prosperous, wealthy and powerful nation. We may live one hundred years and never get the opportunity to do all we want to do or visit all the wonders within our borders. America is a democracy, a country of the free and the brave. It provides us the opportunity, freedom and liberty to shape our personal destiny and that of our nation. We, the people, are responsible for the fate of our nation. The urgency to rebuild the materialistic and social aspects of the USA is now. We have the Means, Will and Reasons. Jobs are being outsourced, manufacturing plants closing, businesses going bankrupt, millions losing jobs and homes, millions in poverty and millions on the verge thereof. The opportunity to create a prosperity greater than the New Deal of the 1930s is present. America has an undeniable destiny, to provide the best for its people and, through leadership, diplomacy and statesmanship, bring prosperity, liberty, freedom and democracy throughout the world. Centuries ago, an American born European colony wanted freedom. America was born. Since then, for most of us, our Hopes and Dreams have been realized and Prayers answered. Millions still hope, dream and pray. Their hopes and dreams will someday be realized and prayers answered. America, with the blessing of GOD, and the Historical Courage and Fortitude of its people, will lead the way. Since 1945 we have spent trillions of our tax dollars throughout the world rebuilding nations and their economies. Tourists have spent trillions more in foreign countries; married millions of foreigners and adopted thousands of foreign babies. Our corporations have outsourced millions of jobs overseas. To achieve our potential, we must create a plan of action so bold that it will lift our people out of poverty and transform America into an even greater nation. A joint local, state, and federal MARSHALL PLAN and REVITALIZATION effort will rebuild our infrastructure, address our social needs, educate our people, increase our resources and strengthen our military, thus allowing us to fulfill our destiny.

Eugenio Macias

PART I: MARSHALL PLAN

PART I: MARSHALL PLAN

Chapter I

Highways, Streets, Tunnels, Drainage, Low Water Crossings

L ocal, state and federal officials constantly divert dedicated taxes and/or are not budgeting for needs. We must increase pressure on those officials to stop the diversion and increase funding. It is time for our elected officials to stop procrastinating and do something, before they have more deaths on their hands.

The majority of our streets are nothing more than asphalt cow paths for vehicles to drive on. As you drive down the streets all you see are rows after rows of houses. Not only is it dangerous for children to play on the streets, but neighbors on one end of the street don't know their neighbors on the other end and cannot keep an eye out for intruders in the neighborhood. Instead of "rowing" the houses, cul-de-sacs should be incorporated into the street design. This allows for neighbors to know neighbors, provides an area for neighbors to get together and for children to play in a safe street environment. To bring our nation together we need to start where American life starts, in the neighborhoods.

Street construction needs to be redesigned in order to reduce travel time, distance traveled, and traffic congestions. Inadequate drainage detrimentally affects street endurance and use. Constantly, drainage pipes burst, requiring repair of pipes and streets. Because local governments grant short term work guarantees to businesses doing the construction or repairs, we the people end up paying the cost of repair after repair. Lack of adequate drainage or even drainage at all is causing constant erosion of streets, extensive damage to vehicles, and fatalities. The antique practice of placing drainage pipes under streets must end. While the inlet to drainage pipes should be on the curbside, the pipes should be under sidewalks, on their side, or even on private property. These actions eliminate having to constantly tear up the streets. Instead of laying utilities underground, cities tend to install utility poles. This not only results in misuse of lumber resources, but is also responsible for many deaths. Governmental lack of action and mismanagement are the major cause of our plight and suffering.

Highway and tunnel systems bear a significant amount of heavy vehicle traffic, causing a constant need for maintenance. Weight and rumbling of those vehicles cause surface damage, and the vibration weakens the structural integrity of the system. Adequate funding and manpower must be provided for continual inspection and repair of the systems. Also, what is needed is to construct parallel highways instead of widening old ones. This is not only less expensive but they can be built faster and can prevent traffic congestion, accidents and frustration. The construction of parallel highways also reduces fuel consumption and wear and tear on vehicles.

Low water crossings are consistently ignored at the local, state and federal level. Where bridges are needed they only put up signs. Yearly, the deaths mount. Pleads for action, by those who suffer the lost of loved ones, fall on deaf ears. It may take the death of a VIP at a crossing to generate priority action.

What we need is a joint local, state and federal effort to eliminate the situation. San Antonio, Texas happens to be the most progressive city in the nation, where national downturns have little effect. Why? San Antonio, with Bond Issues, has embarked on its own Marshall Plan and is improving its infrastructure and addressing social needs. A coordinated effort by major cities, all states and the federal government, following San Antonio's lead, would result in an immediate boost to our economy, job creation and repair of our infrastructure.

Presently, the construction industry is suffering a high level of unemployment. Long term carefully conceived reconstruction programs at all levels of government will generate substantial employment, business opportunities, ease most of our traffic problems, reduce fuel consumption and increase tax revenue.

Chapter II

Bridges, Levees, Dams, Wetlands, Coastal Barriers

N ationwide, bridges, levees and dams are deteriorating at an alarming rate. Again, the diversion by local, state and federal officials of dedicated funds intended to fund repairs, improvements and new construction, has resulted in this deterioration. As a result, the need for more funding has spiraled out of control. Should we fail to act, and act soon, the effect could prove devastating and peril our ability to use the transportation system. We, the people, must engage in forceful action to have our elected officials exercise their responsibilities. We have sat on the sidelines for too long. If we wait any longer, we only have ourselves to blame. Will you be the next one to die when a bridge or dam crumples or a levee breaks? A major problem we have with old bridges is that they are not cost effective to repair. They must be torn down and rebuilt. While low water crossings are the responsibility of counties and cities, the lack of local tax dollars is causing a lack of action. While they can pass bond issues, there still is not enough money available. The federal government needs to provide funding to at least build some bridges over those crossings in order to prevent more deaths. The longer we wait, the higher the cost.

A tiny nation is constructing islands resembling the nations of the world, expanding its shoreline and planning its future for when its oil wells run dry. Why can such a tiny nation plan for its future by engaging in such activities while we cannot even inspect a bridge? Is it because that tiny nation does not engage in wasteful spending and reconstruction of the world?

Some of our wetlands are being devastated by lack of and care-less planning of our dam, levee, coastal barriers and highway sys-tems. There is great need to hasten improvements, before these wet-lands degrade to the point where their rebirth is improbable. Be-cause we allowed coastal barriers to deteriorate, hurricanes continue to destroy our shorelines and coastal cities and towns. To prevent future major destruction as in New Orleans, we must construct new barriers and widen, lengthen, and raise the height of old ones in the Gulf of Mexico and the Pacific and Atlantic Oceans. Our dams are no exception. Not only do we need to repair or reconstruct old ones, we also need to construct new ones in order to increase the avail-ability of our water resource.

Again, a long term, well-conceived reconstruction program will generate substantial economic activity, create employment and ex-pand business opportunities. While some may question the amount of tax revenue used as a result of this program, you must remember that funds spent will recycle several times, thus providing funds for a reasonable portion of the cost.

Chapter III

Dilapidation, Urban Blight, Government Structures

Our infrastructure includes structures such as schools, government buildings, housing, businesses, sports and others. Nationwide, thousands, if not a million or more, are in such sad condition that their demolition is necessary. Many are environmentally dangerous, infested with vermin and used for criminal activity. While some are in isolated locations, most are to be found in poor inner city dilapidating neighborhoods. Because they cause urban blight, investors, businesses and families find it financially unacceptable to build in poor neighborhoods.

Before we revitalize those neighborhoods we must take aggressive action to demolish and/or repair those structures. It should not be only the poor living in those neighborhoods that must demand action, but also people in the affluent areas of the city. Poor neighborhoods create a strain on tax revenue and provide little tax revenue, resulting in higher tax revenue demands on the affluent. Cities throughout the nation need to study what the Avenida Guadalupe Association (AGA) is doing, with scarce revenue, in a poor neighborhood in San Antonio, Texas. Visit. See for yourselves.

I was born in a poor neighborhood. I know first hand that the majority of violent criminals come from those areas. But, by improving poor neighborhoods and the life of the poor you will reduce the criminal population. Poverty and its environment do create the majority of criminals. If we can cause the extinction of plants, animals and insects by destroying their habitat, why can we not destroy the habitat of criminals? We may not be able to do the job 100%, but it would put a substantial dent in criminal growth and activity.

Driving through any major city will find that the majority of government structures are in fluent neighborhoods. Only small branch offices are found in poor neighborhoods. As a result, the wealth in fluent neighborhoods grows while our poor neighborhoods dilapidate. Main government offices in poor neighborhoods would bring businesses, profits, tourism and jobs to those areas. When Senator Obama visited a poor neighborhood in San Antonio, Texas, it generated three months of profits in one day for one business. Likewise, the visit by the Pope in 1987 to the Guadalupe Plaza generated substantial profits for area businesses.

Most do not realize the significant economic impact resulting from the revitalization of inner city poor neighborhoods. It is more than just another program to help the poor. It generates tax revenue at all levels of government, creates jobs and business opportunities, reduces fuel consumption, improves quality of life, eliminates criminal habitats and allows for cities to effectively market themselves. It also leads to a reduction in criminal activity. Bear in mind, poor dilapidating neighborhoods alter many an individuals' perspectives of life, often leading to unacceptable behavior. That unacceptable behavior is the reason for the overcrowding of jails and the millions on probation and parole.

Chapter IV

Transportation, Airports, Jails

On streets and highways people see black smoke pouring out of the tailpipe of vehicles, and others weaving side to side, a clear indication of drunk driving. Yet people refuse to use their cell phones to call the police. In the meantime, because of their inaction, our environment gets polluted and/or someone dies as a result of drunk driving. Get on that phone, place the call, and exercise your responsibility.

We constantly find ourselves in traffic congestion. Many of our streets need to be improved, repaired or reconstructed. There is one helpful solution. In most major cities you find many dead end streets because of gullies, creeks and rivers. Constructing bridges on those streets will help lessen traffic on congested streets. Cities eliminated the use of electric trolleys as a means of transportation and are now using buses. As pollution and the cost for fuel increases, we need to resurrect the use of those trolleys.

Japan and other nations use high speed train systems to transport their people cross country at 200 miles per hour. Across the USA, high speed trains will reduce our use of fuel and the need for more commercial aircraft and buses. It will reduce pollution and traffic congestion. We do not need to expand our airports. It may take longer to travel 1,000 to 2,000 miles by train, but, it is more affordable and a lot more fun than airplanes.

We do not need to construct more "harden criminal" jails. What we need is to construct "hospital jails" to retain and treat drug users and "retention centers" for first time nonviolent offenders. They are the ones increasing our jail population. We need to dissociate them from harden criminals. Rehab for them is impossible in a harden-criminal jail. Dissociate from evil and you will do no evil. Instead of jails turning out more harden criminals, let us do the right thing and provide proper arrangements and treatments for these individuals. Currently, we establish a criminal record for first time nonviolent offenders. This results in them being unable to find a decent paying job. Many of them have turned to criminal activity because of one recorded offense. We need a non-public nonofficial record for first time nonviolent offenders that should be used only by law enforcement and judges if an individual becomes a repeat offender. This record should not be made available to businesses. Give these individuals the opportunity to straighten out, and instead of being a burden, become an asset to society. Remember that businesses no longer give people a second chance.

Chapter V

Water, Lumber, Recycling

N ot enough progress has been made in recycling water, lumber and metal resources. Our growing population and business activity demands more be done. By constructing Salt Water Desalination Plants (SWDP) we can create more of our valuable resources, and expand our ranch and farming industry, thus satisfying our growing needs. Because of droughts, we have millions of uncultivated acres. The Midwest has lost millions of cubic feet of top soil, ranchers and farmers have lost billions in profits and local governments have lost billions in tax revenue. The climate change (higher temperatures) will cause devastating damage to our food resource in the near and far future. We are losing our seashores and a significant amount of agriculture and forest land. The need for SWDP is urgent and essential for the welfare of our nation.

We can construct SWDP in the Pacific to pipe water to the foothills west of the Rockies, to Utah, New Mexico, Nevada, Arizona and California. We can also construct several large lakes in Death Valley which is 230 feet below sea level. These lakes would provide drinking water to the five states and irrigation for some 100,000 square miles of new forest (lumber) and agriculture. We can construct SWDP in the Gulf of Mexico to pipe water east of the Rockies. From there we can pipe drinking water from southwest Texas to South Dakota. We can use the water to refill the 1,000 miles long Ogallala Aquifer, construct lakes, refill the many aquifers that exist in the area, provide for agriculture and create a 200 by

9

1200 miles new forest. We can construct SWDP in the Atlantic to pipe water east of the Appalachians. From here we can pipe drinking and irrigation water throughout the east coast and to many southern states. We can construct several lakes throughout the entire region. We can reduce droughts nationwide.

At the present usage rate we will not have the resources to support a 400 to 600 million population. We must prepare for the future now. The proposed SWDP will increase rainfall, create new springs, bring water to rivers and lakes and reduce the need to irrigate farms, ranches and our lawns. It will increase our ranch and farm yield and provide for the growth of agriculture, including sugar cane, necessary for alternative fuels. It will help purify the air we breathe.

Our government is in no hurry to recycle the airplanes we have in the desert or the rusting ships in graveyards. We have sufficient minerals for the present, but not for the future. We need to cease shipping metal scrapes to foreign nations. We also need to accelerate nationwide the search for more minerals. Our preparations for the future are too limited and extremely slow.

The economic impact of the SWDP would be astronomical. It would have a positive monetary impact on the entire USA, improving our quality of life and lifting millions out of poverty. This action will provide sufficient water and lumber resources to support a doubling of our population.

Chapter VI

Energy, Fuel, Mineral, Ranching, Farming

W e have oil underground in many states, including Alaska and also near our coasts. Yet Congress prohibits oil companies from drilling in many locations. Yes, we need to protect the environment, but, we also need to look at what we need to survive in the future. It appears that only when it becomes prohibitive to drive or fly that disagreeing parties will compromise. We need to retain our underground oil found within the continental USA for future needs. What we need are oil refineries and to drill offshore for oil. The continental oil, offshore oil, hybrid autos, propane gas, high speed trains, electric trolleys and reduction in usage will provide us with fuel for the next two to three hundred years.

Utilities cost is too expensive. We have to reduce use. While "green" housing and business structure construction will help, it is not enough. For now, all new housing should have sky lights, solar water heating and solar power for all small uses. It will allow us to feed energy back into the power grid that can be used to support our industrial base. Research of energy producing products and systems must be accelerated and findings put into service as soon as possible, even if on a piecemeal basis. Overpriced hybrid vehicles reduce gas consumption, but, unless we keep the car for 15–20 years, not our personal expense. We have unknown quantities of minerals underground. Search for these minerals must be accelerated and recycling maximized. Farms and ranches are resources of food. We must find ways to increase their profits in order to prevent owners from selling their land to developers and reducing our agricultural production capability. Developers must find ways and means to construct in inner cities, or as some nations have done, construct underground.

Presently, we are dedicated to using alternative fuels and constructing supplier routes nationwide. What we urgently need is to create an alternative fuel supply and demand in the inner cities. Our ten major cities have some 75,000 taxis and more than 200,000 buses and commercial and public vehicles in daily use. Nationwide, we have more than one million vehicles (taxis, buses, commercial, public, military) in the inner cities that can use propane or alternative fuels. Take care of our urgent concentrated needs first, then expand nationwide.

Immediate actions can reduce fuel consumption and dependency on foreign oil: (1) Federal agencies not essential to the safeguarding of our nation or our safety initiate a ten-hour day, four-day workweek. (2) State and local governments must do the same. (3) Businesses, corporations and organizations not conducting business essential to our health and safety should take the same action. (4) Resurrect the use of electric trolleys. (5) Weather permitting, on military installations, use motor scooters for official business. (6) Weather permitting, on military installations, require security forces to use motorcycles on patrol. (7) All levels of government must require inner city commercial and public vehicles to convert to propane use. (8) The President must create a cross-country high-speed passenger magnetic railroad system similar to the one used in Japan. Several routes are needed, East to West and South to North.

Chapter VII

Technology, Invention

Technologies and inventions reach new heights on a daily basis. But, only those that can afford it can buy them. We must make these new technologies and inventions available to the poor at an affordable cost so that they too can share and participate in our growth. With another fifty million of our population one misstep from poverty, they too may not be able to use these new technologies and inventions. While invention is the creation of a product, technology is the "how" to use it. The computer is the invention of a box that is designed to receive the instruments that carry the technology. Yet, many do not have access to the learning process, all of which cost money they do not have. There are other inventions and technologies that are available to only a few. They must be reduced in price so that the whole nation can profit from them. "Consumer affordable" is fast becoming the key factor as to whether our economy expands or shrinks.

Should I buy a gasoline-only model or a hybrid? The current hybrid I wanted cost $33,000. The quality gasoline only model I bought cost me $17,000. Long term, if the car last that long, the hybrid would have saved me money on gasoline expense. However, I will use the $16,000 saved to travel and enjoy life, and budget the additional $16,000 I need for gas over a twenty-year period. The current hybrid is not consumer affordable. I am also repairing and keeping my paid-off car as a second car. It may cost me $3,000 to repair my car, but it will last me another ten years. Many of us will be doing just that. The industry needs to reduce auto cost, manufacture low-cost fuel efficient autos affordable to the poor and low income, or go out of business. My advice to consumers is to repair your cars, use them, and wait for hybrids that will give you 400 to 600 miles on an electrical charge. That is ten years in the future. Hold off buying a hybrid as long as you can. Question: Do you really need an expensive car, or do you want to buy it just to prove that you have "arrived in high society?" Wouldn't it be better for you to use the "extra" cost (money) to enjoy life? Save your money and travel. See the beauty and all the wonders America offers you. Do all the things you always wanted to. What hybrid auto manufacturers are saying is this, "Pay me the money I save you instead of spending it on gas." Thanks a lot.

There are a number of ways businesses, corporations, banks and financial investment institutions can reduce operating cost. The most important cost reduction step is to stop excessive salary, bonus, incentives and retirement benefits paid their CEO, directors and managers. This action alone can make products "consumer affordable." The $330 million recently paid a CEO to retire from the housing industry confirms the fact that home buyers are paying 10–20% percent more for the house purchased than it is worth. Consumers need to go on a one month strike (purchase only essentials) to force corporations to take corrective action, and as a way of informing corporations of what they can expect in the future. That includes the auto industry.

Chapter VIII

People, National Parks, Government

The greatest resource that America has is its people. Yet, we only effectively use those that have access to higher education. We have no reliable method to find the high capacity, or geniuses, that exist in the ranks of the poor. The poor are not holding America back. America is holding the poor back. Instead of helping educate our children, American businesses import educated legal immigrants and pay them lower wages. Hire our college graduates at prevailing salaries. Our high school and college students should descend on Washington, D.C. demanding that this type of legal immigration be abolished.

Our national parks are marvels to be enjoyed. They are well managed. But, as our population grows and more tourists visit the sites, it seems as if there are no plans as to how best to manage future situations. Many of us may be denied entrance to these parks because they are packed to capacity or visit the sites on a stay-on-the-bus tour. One partial solution is to alternate the school year among states so that tourists can visit April through September instead of June through August.

Our government is a resource. Our problem is that an elected politician's main concern is reelection, and not the well being of our people. Some politicians have become too powerful and need to be removed. One glaring example is the chairmen of committees that refuse to allow certain bills to be presented for further action. These rejected bills are submitted to fulfill a purpose and deserve to be heard by all elected officials. One politician alone should not be allowed that power. Voters must remove them from office. Government is a resource for us to use in order for us to prosper in our individual endeavors, and should not be used by politicians to empower themselves. Another example is one subject to debate. The Mexican government, illegal immigrants, drug traffickers, oil companies, businesses and corporations can be blamed for many of our problems. Those most responsible for the problems we face today live in our backyard, Congress and the President. The power they have inherited has caused their mental capacity to collapse, resulting in their inability to use common sense and to act in the manner necessary for us to prosper as individuals and as a nation. Our local, state and federal governments have proven to be mindless resources.

Chapter IX

Low/Middle Income, Poverty, Homeless, Housing, Obesity

O nce I was one of the poorest of the poor. I had my own 10'X10' garden where I grew vegetables to supplement whatever my mother could afford to buy with her income from ironing, baby sitting, cooking and house cleaning. If there was welfare then, my mother refused it. She would accept help, but never money. That upbringing shaped my views. I do not support monetary life supporting systems, including the income tax credit for the poor. If they need help with food, medicine, medical, shelter, transportation or education, help provide them with the essentials. But, no money. For the low income (not poorest of the poor) we need to create life support programs where we partially assist them with in-kind programs that will improve their ability to provide for themselves. But, no money. The granting of money is one major reason for our federal deficit (debt).

Our local, state and federal welfare systems need an overhaul. I have met single parent women drawing welfare benefits and food stamps that are not in poverty. These women claim poverty status because of being single, having a low income and dependent children. They use food stamps when in fact they have undeclared income earning common-law husbands (johns), drive new vehicles, own expensive TVs, stereos and other furnishings and use money for liquor and cigarettes. Some have arrived in Cadillac's, Lexus, RVs and SUVs at centers to collect their share of free school supplies and clothing. There are other aspects that reveal they are not in poverty. But, welfare agencies do not have the means, funds and manpower to investigate.

After the wealthy, it is the "middle income" that pay too much in income tax. Some tax programs actually penalize them. Being middle income does not mean that they can afford to purchase all their needs. Businesses and financial institutions are not interested in making a buck, not as long as they can gouge them to death. But, the middle income can 'turn the tables' on them. Do not use credit cards unless you can pay the entire amount on a monthly basis. If you can, divide your monthly mortgage payment in two and make twice a month payments. And if you can afford it, increase the amount of your payment by $10 or $20. These two actions will reduce a thirty-year fix rate mortgage to fifteen years. If you have an expensive whole life insurance plan, terminate it and obtain a less costly term life insurance plan. Obtain a prepaid funeral plan. Unless you are a spendthrift, you will find that you can save a substantial amount of money for your retirement. Instead of buying an expensive vehicle, buy a good quality but less expensive one. I did. Afterwards I spent ten vacations in the Philippines. Do not get in over your head because of a fast talking salesman who wants to make an extra buck.

I do not support bail out programs for all individuals that lost their homes. Many are sinking in credit card debt and making payments on expensive cars, boats, swimming pools, TVs, stereos, appliances, furniture, and sending their children to private schools. Help the innocence, not the big spenders. Live high on the hog, suffer the consequences.

People look down on the homeless. I don't. There, but for the grace of God, go I. Homelessness is not a social problem. It is an untapped resource wandering the streets of America. Yes, a very few of them are nothing more than worthless scum. For most it was just one or two missteps, and boom, they became homeless. If one or two missteps lead them into homelessness, one or two steps of kindness (help) can lead them back to prosperity.

Investors and overpaid CEOs drive up the price of a house, not supply and demand. Anyone who has experienced a 10–20% reduction in the value of their house paid more than its value when they bought the house. The lesson to be learned by home buyers is if you cannot afford a fixed mortgage rate, do not buy. If you cannot negotiate the price down by 10–20%, don't buy. Just wait. Developers will come knocking on your door begging you to buy the house. Instead of buying, obtain a lease with option to buy. In two years faulty construction will reveal itself. Lose a few thousand dollars in rent money, not tens of thousands on a house with a warranty worded so that developers are not liable for faulty construction. If businesses and financial institutions want to stay in business, they will come to terms with you. Use reason, not emotion, when buying. The problem is that most of you "want it now."

Obesity is a billion-dollar industry. Full-body men and women are more attractive than skinny ones. You must talk to your doctor first, then try these simple solutions: eat six snacks of food rather than three big meals; eat less pork, meat, chicken, fish and potatoes; eat more fresh fruit and fresh vegetables; drink pure juices and not those made from concentrates, during the winter season spend some time in the sun; run short and walk long distances; eat dinner before 7:00 P.M.; run around inside the house during TV commercials; do exercises that do not require equipment; walk more and drive less. To gain endurance and vitality, eat fresh broccoli and drink two ounces of Aloe Vera juice and a teaspoon of pure bee honey daily. If doing this doesn't help, then spend your money on doctors, pills, operations and exercise equipment.

You must, I repeat, must, talk to your doctor on these two before you decide to incorporate them into your personal health program. Apple cider vinegar is a blood thinner. On and off over the past 20 years I have: (1) mixed apple cider vinegar with pure bee honey (50/50 mix), and drank a tablespoon daily; (2) mixed aloe vera juice with apple juice (50/50 mix) and drank four ounces daily. I have had no side effects, and I feel very energized. Do not do it at night as you will be too energized to go to sleep.

The giving away of tax dollars by any means (grants, tax loopholes, income tax credits, etc.) is having an impact on the growth of our federal deficit (debt). Loans, yes. Grants, no. Let me use the low income housing grant program as an example. Suppose I am low income and obtain a $25,000 grant (down payment assistance) to purchase a house. At current interest rates, depending on my years of life, that grant may be worth $100,000 when I die. My children are doctors, accountants and store managers, and my children in law, are managers, directors, teachers and nurses. When I die, they inherit the house, including the $100,000. They should have no rights to that money. I suggest that we convert that grant program to a loan program and make the loan due and payable when I die. When the loan is made, a permanent lien is placed on that house. Recycling that money allows us to help other low income families in the future. The loan program will help reduce the federal deficit because we get our money back to use in assisting other poor families. Under the current grant system, the more money we pour into the program the greater the need for more money. It is an incurable disease that never dies.

Chapter X

Abuse, Adoption, Abortion

A buse of children, women, elderly and even men, is a growing menace. Yet people, seeing or experiencing the abuse, close their eyes and remain silent. Eliminate the fear of taking the appropriate action to stop the abuses. Reduce the abusive environment. Yes, government officials need to be better trained to handle abusive situations. However, it will never be enough if adequate funding is not provided to increase agency manpower. The under staffing of the agencies is the major reason for case worker burn out and inadequacy in handling abusive cases. To top it off, our home is now our refuge, where neighborly association is extinct. We close the doors and lock out the world.

Where can a child find love, wanting, joy and security other than at home with loved ones? Adoption centers do provide some of that. However, it is not enough. A child belongs in a home with loving parents. Yet, while our adoptable children remain in adoption centers, Americans run around the world adopting children. Children that get adopted in the states are lucky simply because it is very expensive to adopt and care for a child. Why should we adopt a child when we can get paid to "foster care" a child? My choice would be fostering care. At least I would be able to provide that child with love and a home environment. It hurts me that millions of children die yearly in foreign lands. But, that is no reason for us to abandon or forsake our own orphans to a childhood with no parents and no love.

Clearly, the law needs to be changed in favor of adopting a child rather than foster care. It would be less expensive if states were to use their own lawyers and agencies and establish a college fund for an adopted child. The states should pay that child's medical expenses as it costs less than health insurance. (Few children need costly medical care before the age of 18). Less case workers would be needed and child care centers would be emptied. Adoptive parents could then afford to provide room, board, security, family stableness and love. We have an even greater problem. As our population grows so do the number of orphans. It will not end until abusive parents become more responsible. That is not going to happen.

As long as many of us turn our backs on our faith we will continue to have abortions. We can forever argue as to at what point after conception does a fetus become a human being. Is abortion murder, or is it the discarding of an unwanted fetus? Not being God, I cannot answer that question. If a woman becomes pregnant, at least allow that child to be born. If the child is unwanted by the birth mother, the least society can do for that child is to provide for it the best it can. My personal opinion is that humanity begins the instance of conception. Think before you abort, for where there is life, there is hope.

Chapter XI

Law, Crime, Justice

The substantial majority of criminals are created by the environment society has spun. The most prominent factor creating a criminal is poverty. Having to decide which to pay first, rent, utilities, food or medicine, or going hungry, having no money to pay doctors or for medicines, lack of education and living in slums creates criminals. In addition, businesses not giving first time non-violent offenders a second chance is creating criminals. What else can they do, if they cannot earn a living?

Stop relying solely on the police capturing and incarcerating criminals. Get to know your neighbors. Associate with your neighbors. As I grew up, I found friends helping friends, neighbors helping neighbors. If not for friends, neighbors, and a stern mother, what would my life be like today if I had accepted the offer of a Westside drug territory instead of joining the military? What would have become of me if it weren't for friends being there in my times of need? Most can overcome heart breaking situations, if you provide your friendship in time of their need.

The consistent misapplication of law by the justice system has resulted in unjustified sentencing of criminals. For the same offense, individuals of different ethnic groups and/or social standing receive different sentences. We have two arrogant laws. If you are a drug trafficker and you get caught, your possessions are confiscated and you go to jail for twenty years. If you are a millionaire and you commit a criminal act (embezzling $100 million, price fixing or manipulate stocks), you keep the money, your possessions and you go home to your family and mansion, in your Mercedes Benz. Some laws need to be changed. And judges need to be scrutinized as concerns their decisions.

When an individual commits a crime, our first instinct is to put him in jail. However, the jail is nothing more than a hotel suite with free everything: room, food, cable television, gym, and library. They even get a free college education. We are the ones in jail, not them. We install dead bolt locks, window bars and alarm systems in our homes and places of business. We escort our children to and from school. To protect ourselves, we are buying guns like never before. So what do we continue doing? We continue putting more people in poverty and creating more criminals.

I am a Christian, of high moral character. But, I can face facts. We are wasting money and causing deaths fighting drug usage and trafficking, and prostitution. It is a futile battle without end. Legalize drugs and prostitution, and then tax them. They are less expensive to treat and control than to fight. It reduces criminal activity and associated deaths. Legalizing alcohol and gambling proved that. Christians need to come to their senses. A major step we can take to reduce drug usage is to require drug tests for all who apply for a marriage license and benefits of any kind (grants, loans, welfare, food stamps, etc.). Do what is necessary. Try to criminalize the private commission of adultery, fornication, masturbation, cursing and using the Lords' name in vain. The commission of sin is payable to God. The commission of crime is payable to you. You need more local tax revenue? Why send your gambling dollars to Las Vegas? Legalize gambling in your state, create jobs and use the tax dollars for your benefit. If you are concerned about the poor wasting their money gambling, think twice. Many of them are spending money in Las Vegas, playing bingo, buying lottery tickets and betting on illegal cock fights. Christians, Christians, Christians. Render onto the Lord what is the Lords.' Render onto you what is yours.

Chapter XII

General, Technical, Vocational Education

S tudy hard, learn, and apply yourself. Go to college. Become a professional. You can do it. However, instead of having students learn we teach them how to pass test after test. When they fail, society hollers that the school system is responsible. Passing exams does not prepare a student for college. Learning does. And when they do earn admission to a college they find that they passed exams but didn't learn and that funds are not available for them to attend and/or complete a four-year college. Stop blaming teachers for student failures. Blame those responsible, parents, system, environment and politicians. The current school year is 170 days out of 365. A whole year of school will still be only 225 days out of 365. We have some ten school districts where one or two will suffice. Just don't tell that to entrenched school board members.

We do not need to import immigrant teachers. We have a surplus on hand. The problem we have is that they quit their profession to get a better job or become stay at home mothers. I do not blame them. Why should they put up with the burdens we place on them, such as excessive reports, unruly children, students on drugs, use them as policemen and reduce their power and authority? Requiring students to pass an exit exam and refusing to grant them a diploma is stupid. All we are doing is creating another obstacle to their future.

We should provide poor children at least a full two-year tuition scholarship at a community college. If they pass muster, provide them with another two-year scholarship at the nearest four-year college. Not everyone needs to attend an expensive college or university. Maybe then we will not have to import doctors, nurses, teachers and scientists.

Forget the "you can do it" college education myth. Not everyone, poor or rich, has the mental ability to obtain a college degree. That does not mean they do not have the mental ability or capacity to receive technical and vocational training. Amongst others, we need nurses' aids, construction workers, mechanics, air-condition experts, plumbers and electricians. But, most of the poor do not have the financial means to get the training needed. A vocational or technical scholarship for them would go a long way in reducing our shortage of skilled workers. My friend served on active duty in a nuclear submarine, has an IQ of 142, Masters in business and specializes in business and stock investments. Yet, he has been unable to find a job.

We are producing too many individuals with law, business, marketing and other degrees for which they cannot find a comparable job. Yet they are intelligent enough to be rocket engineers and scientists. They have wasted their time and money. At the same time we are having to import educated immigrant scientists, mathematicians, doctors, nurses, teachers and engineers. Our students either are being misdirected, not receiving appropriate counseling, are unknowledgeable of the situation, or are not effectively researching future job opportunities. Parents, teachers, counselors, brothers, sisters, uncles and aunts need to communicate more effectively, in order to discovery the true potential of a child.

Some of the reasons for the high college drop out rates are that students are partying instead of learning, getting high on drugs and alcohol, and trying to sow their (girls and boys) oaks. When children return home on school breaks, parents should require them to take drug tests. College officials should also have as a requirement for admission that students take a drug test before admission and random tests thereafter.

It is amazing that America, the most progressive and advanced nation in the world, is a nation where the majority of its people speak one language. In progressive nations and in some third world countries people are fluent in two or more languages. Today a bilingual or trilingual person is a foreigner. A one-lingual person is an American. Are we ever going to start preparing our children for the future?

Chapter XIII

Small Businesses, Immigration, Minimum/Living Wages

S mall businesses are the life support system of the American economy, producing the majority of jobs and keeping the American economy growing. They support the majority of American families. So the government decides to reduce the Small Business Administration budget. As a result fewer small businesses are created and many more fall by the wayside. Our economy will continue to grow, but not enough to fulfill our needs. While Congress has reduced the SBA budget, hundreds, if not thousands, of nonproductive government-funded agencies and nonprofit organizations continue being funded.

We desperately need an Unskilled World Guest Worker Program. Few American born will accept almost-slave wages or do "dirty" jobs, especially when they have families. They rather accept government welfare. I do not support amnesty for illegal immigrants (stop calling them undocumented). Why, after we granted them amnesty, are millions of illegal immigrants not working the harvest? We can have a very effective guest worker program. It will forgive the illegal for illegal crossing, but require all unemployed illegal immigrants to return home (if we have to deport them, they cannot come back under the guest worker program). The program will also require that American employers determine the need for workers and advertise. If local workers are still not found, they can apply to a foreign employment agency for workers, an agency which screens applicants and provides them a ten-year American contract. The contract will have several specifications: workers return home upon completion of the contract; workers cannot bring family and will not be allowed to become US citizens; US employers will deduct medical insurance cost (not Medicare) from that workers pay; US employers will deduct income tax from that workers pay; US employers will deduct social security taxes from that workers pay; when the workers return home those funds will be paid to them in total; should they become US citizens, and stay in the US, those funds will be deposited into our social security program; we reserve the option to offer them citizenship at the completion of their contract. This program will allow for manageable growth of our population, while leaving the door open to citizenship for those who earn it. Also, we should allow employers of illegal immigrants the opportunity to obtain visas for those currently employed that have proven to be an asset to the company. We should allow employers to request visas for guest workers by name.

However, the guest worker program should be only for industries needing unskilled workers (janitors, waitresses, harvest, etc.). Industries, such as construction, that offer good opportunities and pay, must not be allowed to use this program. We must not allow the guest worker program to take good jobs from citizens willing to do the work.

A guest worker program and modern technology will help reduce illegal crossings, drug trafficking and the terrorist threat. But, it is not enough. Illegal crossings will continue as long as the corrupt Mexican government does nothing for its people in order to stop the flow. A fence is essential, but only in parts of and not the entire border. We must face reality. We are not the size of China. Our resources cannot support a population of three billion. We must reduce the legal and illegal immigration if we are to provide for ourselves and our future population. Legal and illegal immigration affects American wages. Due to our politicians' lack of foresight, the minimum wage remains a constant battle. The minimum wage should be for teenagers. Adults, whether single or married, have different needs and should be paid a living wage or salary. Teenagers spend their money mainly on themselves. Adults venture out, get married, pay rent or mortgage, and pay for their medical, food, clothing and entertainment. Minimum wages for adults mean eternal poverty.

Chapter XIV

Race/Color/Census

B ecause of our upbringing, feelings and emotions, whether or not we want to admit it, many of us, the elderly, find it difficult to rid ourselves of our discriminating and prejudice feelings. We may not say it out loud, but we do mutter our thoughts to ourselves. It just so happens that we are dying off. Most of our children, grandchildren, and great grandchildren do not share our views, feelings, and emotions when it comes to race and color. Our children have learned or are learning that the inside of a person is more important than race, religion or color when choosing someone to love and/or be friends with.

Marriage between people of different race and/or color is a common occurrence. Mix marriages will multiply in the near and far future. Except for immigrants, there will be no ethnic or race categorization of people. The future America will be theirs and their children's world. In the not too distant future it will be difficult for the census forms to list people by race or color. The census, when taken, will list one characteristic for the American born, American. Also, the terms Anglo, African American, Hispanic, and Asian will be eliminated.

The census is taken for three reasons. The first is to count the number of people. The second one is for businesses to determine how best to advertise to people of different color, race, religion, gender and age. Those businesses that advertise in Spanish are wasting their money. Most second generation, and beyond, Spanish heritage people cannot read, write or speak Spanish (they may know Tex-Mex). They buy American style, not the way their parents and grandparents from their old country did. The third reason is for Congress to determine how to dole out welfare benefits and how to appeal to their voters in order to win reelection.

Our future Americans are being born today and they are color and race blind. America is no longer a melting pot where individuals retain their ethnic identification and melt into society. America is becoming a nation where the co-mingling of blood will be the natural order of life. There will be no single-blooded individuals in America's future. That is reality. In 2007 there were five million American children born into mixed marriage families. By 2030 there will be thirty million, by 2060 sixty million and by 2150 all will be co-mingled blooded American citizens. By 2150 there will be no Anglos, Asians, Blacks or Hispanics. Only Americans.

Chapter XV

Military, Police, Firemen, Emergency Medical Personnel

O ur military is strong in courage and bravery, but weak in equipment, manpower, benefits, and proper utilization. Yes, we remain the most powerful nation in the world. However, after every war, every President has reduced our military strength in size and equipment. No matter how you look at it, reducing our military capability is the most ignorant action taken by our government. We need an active military force of two million. Our reserves and National Guard should be placed on active duty only when it is absolutely necessary, as when our two million force is overwhelmed. Why do we not reduce the number of our troops overseas in half, and require our allies to provide the other half? I found the answer. All our presidents have decided that we are the World Police. Where does USA responsibility end and allied and UN responsibilities begin?

Someone came up with the idea that we needed to consolidate (BRAC) our military in order to reduce cost. As a result, one bomb will destroy our logistic air force base, Warner Robin. Kelly AFB has been closed. One bomb will destroy Brooke Army Medical Center. Wilford Hall Medical Center is downsizing, if not closed altogether. We have reduced the number of targets that the enemy has to destroy to render us helpless, just to save a buck. Centralization and concentration may be smart moves for businesses, but not for our military.

While the percentage of crimes committed may decrease, the

number increases as a result of population growth. But the police force is not top priority for most city and state governments, in number or compensation. In the end, do we want to be sorry and not safe, or do we want to be safe and not sorry? We holler every time police do not respond immediately. And we holler every time they get proper pay and equipment. In every city, the police department must be the number one priority, adequately paid, equipped and manned.

Firemen and Emergency Medical personnel are also underpaid and undermanned. We holler when the response is not immediate and our house burns to the ground. And there is no one around to tell firemen that inside the house and garage we have gasoline, oil, propane, paint and other flammable liquids. And we blame the firemen for not putting out the fire before it consumed the entire house? Consider the dilemma of emergency medical personnel. The majority of the calls they reply to are non-emergencies. They cannot find your house because the address is not visible. People have no idea what they did recently that may be the cause of their condition. Many do not know what medicines they are taking. Many will not admit that they drank liquor before or after they took their medicine. And it goes on and on. If your local taxes are increased, please don't cry. What we want from our military, police, firemen and emergency medical personnel is the whole pie, but we only want to pay for a slice.

Most nations of the world have a need for America's help. But, we have two friendly nations that need our help, and we need theirs, Mexico and the Philippines. We have the immediate need for two or more active duty army brigades. They have intelligent, healthy and physically fit young men and women who have a command of the English language. We can offer them American citizenship. What we would require from them is a ten-year active duty commitment, with all the entitlements and benefits we offer our own. At the end of the ten-year term, they automatically become US citizens. We fill ours and their urgent needs. Their urgent needs are that they need to help their families back home and provide for the education of their brothers and sisters. One incidental benefit for us is that we would earn (instead of buy) the friendship of thousands of their family members. Each individual that we help has, in his extended family, at least 100 members. If they marry someone from back home, their extended family increases to 200. We need all the friends overseas that we can get.

You will be surprised at what you can find reading books, newspapers, magazines, listening to the radio, watching TV and other sources. It took one leading Filipino politician to create hatred for America in a few politicians and a few ordinary civilians. The substantial population of Filipinos would love to have our military forces back. Our military presence, especially in Iraq, has created hatred for the USA amongst Muslims. True? Yes. Iran is an evil nation. True? Yes. But, that applies mainly to the leadership. The substantial majority of ordinary Iranians want democracy and good relations with America. Instead of trying to convince the "evil" leadership to become "good guys," we should be encouraging the ordinary Iranians to take action and change their leadership. A change in our foreign policy by exercising leadership and extending friendship to Iranian citizens may prove more effective than the threat of war. We do not need to change Muslims. What we need is for them to remove extreme idiots from leadership. We also need to do that in Venezuela.

Chapter XVI

Medical, Medicine, Medicare

O ur medical, Medicare and medicine systems are out of whack
and getting worse. For the poor and the elderly it is a disaster.
For the middle income it is becoming a disaster. Talk is about
a federal program that will cost billions and benefit millions. Yet,
we do not know who or how many are sick, of what and the cost.
We first need a federal preventive health program that will provide
for the medical examination (physical for the disabled only) of
families with an annual gross income of less than $150,000. Only
when we know what the situation really is should we create a health
treatment program for them. We need to remove the Medicare tax
cap so that we can afford medical programs. Why should only the
poor and middle income pay Medicare tax on 100% of their income? Do you buy a used car without first inspecting it? Do you
buy a pre-owned house without a licensed inspector inspecting it
first? I don't. We need to do the same for health programs. We have
millions of children without health insurance. That is true. I also
know that the majority of them do not need to see a doctor every
year and may not need to see one for ten or fifteen years. It may be
cheaper to pay their medical expenses rather than make insurance
companies richer, with our tax dollars. Where is the common sense?

Hospitals and clinics are closing all over the nation, mostly because of unpaid services to illegal immigrants and a lack of doctors
and nurses. We urgently need the guest worker program previously
mentioned. There is one action, and one action only, that needs to

be taken and taken immediately in order to force our elected officials to pass effective legislation. Cities nationwide need to start rounding up and deporting the illegal. The outcry will be phenomenal. The actions I call for are beneficial not only to the illegal, but also to us. By forcing, and I mean forcing, our government to enact an effective immigration program we will be protecting ourselves, and finally bringing humanitarian justice to illegal immigrants. You may say I am being cruel. If that is your opinion, it is because you did not study my guest worker program.

We need doctors and nurses (teachers too). So what we do is import them. While doing so, we do not educate many gifted and talented low and middle income children that can fill those voids. Because our government is so busy finding ways to waste our tax dollars, it cannot afford to fund our children's education. Wasting minds is a pitiful exercise of our educated elected ignoramus officials.

Chapter XVII

Taxation, Deficit, Social Security, Line Item Veto

We constantly hear about taxation, the deficit, the use of the line item veto, and social security. Nothing is ever done and nothing really changes, except that in the near future we may have to work until the age of 100 before we can collect social security (and Medicare) benefits. Not one politician has had the courage and conviction to submit a bill setting a cut off date of the present personal and business tax systems, and establishing a start date of new systems. It does not matter. They are too inept and too obligated to "special interest" to agree on a fair system. What is a fair system? One that modifies the present system, or is it a simple one sheet system? Neither one is fair.

The almost paperless personal tax system needed is to deduct a certain percentage rate for taxes, based on anticipated earnings and other income, and for employers and financial institutions to report all income earned and tax deducted directly to the IRS. Once all the income is reported, the IRS will determine the applicable percentage rate. If the individual was overtaxed, it refunds the difference. If the individual was under-taxed, it will forward a bill and collect the difference. Everybody pays their applicable tax rate, regardless of income or where the income came from. No tax loopholes. No matter how rich or poor one may be, each person earning an income pays their individual tax, regardless if one is single, married, divorced or has one to ten children. The lower the income, the lower the percentage tax rates. It is that simple. The starting percentage rate should be 1% for those earning less than $10,000. No taxation, no representation.

The business tax system is a mess. Enough said. Since the IRS is undermanned, the business tax return may never get audited. The business tax system must be reformed and loopholes eliminated, especially those enacted for special interest groups. But, do not expect any changes to the system as politicians are beholden to special interest groups and corporations. The biggest government lie is that the federal deficit is $9 trillion. The true amount is in excess of $60 trillion when you include unpaid interest and government benefits. That translates into $180,000 for every man, woman and child.

In addition to a fair personal and business income tax, the federal government must create a 1% sale tax on all luxury items. Not only would the wealthy pay this tax, but so would wealthy visitors to our nation. The purpose of this tax is to help pay off the federal deficit (debt). When the deficit (debt) is eliminated, the tax is discontinued. To further reduce the deficit Congress needs to start complying with GAO findings in order to stop wasteful spending. There are thousands of agencies and nonprofit organizations that need to be terminated, and thousands more audited to determine their continuation.

Ah, social security. The retirement age was raised in order to save tax dollars. Some citizens receiving benefits in foreign countries have died, but friends and relatives are cashing their checks. The poor and middle income pay social security (and Medicare) taxes on 100% of their income. Why is it that the wealthy do not? Because of the high number of baby boomers getting ready to retire there are fears that no funds will be left in the social security system to pay benefits at the current rate. Nonsense. The majority of baby boomers were high on drugs and alcohol during their early age. Many still are. Others have contracted AIDS. My fear of the system running out of money is lessened because a high percentage of them will die before they turn 80, all because of their indiscretion. Obesity will kill many more. Do we have enough cemetery space? No pun intended.

The line item veto is another of those much talked about, and nothing ever done. And unless politicians commit themselves, before we vote for them, nothing will ever be done. We can always

recall them, and try again with others. While some of the pork barrel projects are actually deserving projects, most are pure pork.
Without the line item veto nothing can or will ever be done to stop
wasteful spending. By putting pressure on politicians now, today,
we can reduce the federal budget. We just need a majority to get the
job done. If we the people do not take forceful action and bring
pressure to bear on politicians the systems will never be fixed and
the federal deficit will continue growing and growing and growing.

I am neither poor nor wealthy. But! I did a curiosity study of
the rich. They pay a good percentage of our tax revenue. I calcu-
lated that if we do not increase their tax rate, and quadruple the
number of our billionaires and millionaires and their wealth, we can
eliminate the personal income tax paid by the poor and middle income. What a revolting idea.

Chapter XVIII

Pollution, Environment

Pollution affects the environment. Environment affects pollution. Because of normal cycles the environment is responsible for climate change, both hot and cold. Because of man-made pollution the climate changes, both hot and cold, on a daily basis. But the pollution we create damages the environment, sometimes beyond repair, and is responsible for current day extinctions. Currently, scientists blame either one or the other for the present weather pattern. What they refuse to acknowledge is that the normal environmental cycle and pollution have joined forces, with drastic results. What can be done that will have the immediate impact that will result in an acceptable weather pattern?

Three things must happen. First, reduce pollution output. Second, we have to plant billions of trees worldwide to replace deforestation. Third, we need to plant more greenery in our yards and countryside. (I have been ridiculed on one of my ideas. We have air purifiers in homes to purify indoor air. Why can we not purify air outdoors with large air purifiers at or near plant polluting areas and in heavy city and other congested traffic areas)? These three actions will result in a significant reduction of pollutants. The problem is that we wait on governments to act instead of doing what we need to do, and forcing politicians to take action.

In my 13,000 square feet yard I have planted six trees, created three small vegetable gardens and one flower garden. I planted three orange trees (one died). I also grow my own peanuts and grapes.

Drought, pollutants, and climate warming affect everything. In 2007 we grew 500 tomatoes; in 2008 we may get 50. In 2007 we grew 600 oranges, and in 2008 we have none. We grew six bushels of grapes in 2007. In 2008 we might get one bushel. My banana trees, with fruit, are dying. Onions, radishes, peppers, string beans and my wife's Filipino vegetables are OK. The cucumbers are flowering but not producing. Last year we had rain. Not this year.

Pollutants enter our aquifers, rivers, lakes and oceans mainly because of insufficient manpower to policy polluting industries and businesses. The Environmental Protection Agency (EPA) gets blamed for slow and insufficient action. The truth is that lack of funds and shortage of manpower does not allow it to take the actions we need and demand. Instead of blaming them, blame Congress and the President for they are the ones who lack foresight and fortitude.

Chapter XIX

Foreign Military, Economic Aid

O ur foreign military and economic aid programs are a disgrace. We get drawn into military action in nations with weapons obtained from the US or from our allies. We want weapon control, yet we have no accountability for the weapons "lost" in Korea, Viet Nam, Afghanistan, Iraq and even from our armories. What we do know is that many are in the hands of dictators, despots, rebels and in nations where someday we will need to take military action. We do not have an effective weapon accountability program. Our foreign military aid program and foreign intervention (World Police) mostly benefit the US weapon production industry. We need to evaluate our military aid. Instead of arming nations, we should pursue a disarmament policy. All nations should maintain an effective police force. There is no need for small nations to maintain an army, especially if the UN creates nonaggression treaties between neighboring nations and establishes a UN military intervention force.

We have poured millions, if not billions, of economic dollars into nations who refuse to account for them. We are using the economic aid program to buy the support and friendship of nations, and their vote in the UN. We have not earned their friendship and support. This aid program needs a serious audit, and reduction of funds. What we really need is to provide the UN with specific funds, and let it provide the economic support.

Should we continue with a foreign economic aid policy it

should be modified. For accountability purposes, instead of granting funds to governments, we should directly contract and pay for economic improvement projects in the nations we assist. For example, many nations in the Middle East have limited water sources, especially those bordering the Sahara Desert. A salt water desalination plant could provide water to several nations. This water could be used for agriculture, thus providing people the ability to feed themselves. We could directly contract for insect and vermin eradication projects, such as mosquitoes and rats. Because foreign politicians put foreign aid money in their pockets, their people do not respect or support us. Continuing the current policy is not in our best interests.

I do not believe in isolationist policies for America. But, I believe it is time for us to drastically reduce or temporally suspend foreign economic aid and use that money for our urgent needs.

Chapter XX

Foreign, Local Humanitarian Aid

In nations with good governments, and where disaster strikes, humanitarian aid is welcomed and distributed to the needy. In nations with dictators and despot rulers, and where disaster strikes, humanitarian aid normally ends up in hands of the rulers, and is not distributed to the needy. Yet, we refuse to take the action required to ensure that the needy receive the aid provided. We may need to take dictators, despots and rebels head-on. If that is what is required, then we must do it. We cannot allow for the death of millions at the hands of a few.

In the US, because of rising sea levels, New Orleans, which is ten feet below sea level, will be twenty feet under water before we provide all the Katrina promised aid. Some towns in and around New Orleans were wiped off the map. What is the status of all the people caught in hurricane Katrina's path? How many more years before they receive aid? We are quick to provide aid to foreign nations, and slow to provide it at home. Our national humanitarian aid program needs serious review. We must provide our people aid, and we need to provide it when needed.

I was amazed with the audacity of the insurance companies in refusing to pay Louisiana homeowners for water damage to their homes because they had no "flood" insurance. They pulled a fast one on the homeowners and the city, state and federal governments. What happened in New Orleans was that the hurricane was responsible for the levees to break. No hurricane, no levee breakage and no flooding.

What we need is a major insurance company to conceive an all-inclusive nationwide house insurance policy that will pay home-owners for whatever damages their homes, other than owner inflicted damages. The same rate should be applied nationwide, but adjusted to local replacement cost. Spreading insurance cost nationwide for a particular damage will benefit all, including the insurance companies. This type of an all-inclusive insurance policy would have allowed insurance companies to pay for all the housing damage caused by hurricane Katrina. Federal income tax revenue would not have been needed except for infrastructure repairs. Study this concept. Do the math. It will do the job.

Chapter XXI

Consumer Rip-Off

C onsumer rip-off is a mainstay of our life. I will use auto repairs as an example that can be applied to most anything. In my youth I prepared autos for painting, and painted them. Recently, I was involved in a car accident. Because of unreasonable high cost (three estimates) for repairs my car was "totaled" by the insurance company. Mechanically, nothing is wrong with it. To paint two bumpers the average labor cost was 11.7 hours @ $38.00 = $442.87 and paint supplies cost was 11.7 hours @ 26.66 = $314.27, total $757.14. From my experience the required labor was 2 hours @ $38.00 = $76.00 and paint supplies, not in hours but in supplies, $10.00. With a 100% profit mark up the total cost should have been $172.00. Ironically, the bumpers only needed rubbing compound and wax. Subsequent inspection (by me) revealed the bumpers were not damaged by the accident.

A suit at one store cost $250. The same suit at another store cost substantially more. The actual selling price for a garment is $25. The store selling price is $50, but, offers you a 50% discount. There are several reasons stores can offer you discounts. One is to get you to buy higher priced items. Another is to get rid of excess merchandise. Even with a 75% discount, the stores still make money. Another one is that enough suckers paid an artificially high price when the products first came out. You can buy a car with a high mileage warranty. However, the cost of the warranty is included in the sales price. That same warranty may cost less at a warranty company. To prevent you from invalidating the warranty, you are required to have non-essential expensive maintenance done at specific mileage. Currently, any new house you buy is overpriced 10–20% because of investor purchases and CEO incentives, not supply and demand. Most new house warranties are written so as to minimize developer cost and increase buyers cost for faulty construction. Costly breakdowns of most anything manufactured will occur after the warranty expires.

You constantly receive notices "Overstocked. Must sell 500 cars. Profit doesn't matter. Highest trade in for your car. $10,000, $15,000 discount on select models. Etc., etc., etc."

Get your magnifying glass and read the small print. Without intentions of buying, I have attended several of these events. My findings? Everyone I attended was a rip-off, designed to get me to the dealership and extract money from my pocket. Have you received one of those no payments, no interest for X number of years advertisements? Buy? Remember, the interest is included in the sale price. If you don't pay it off in the prescribed period, you end up paying more interest. Department stores credit cards. Get one and get 10% discount on your first purchase. When you receive the bill, pay it off in full. Then call and cancel the card. If you don't, you will incur extremely high interest rates. "They" increased your credit card limit? Call and say "no, thank you." Remember, housing developers, department stores, auto dealerships and financial institutions don't care about you, or your family. All these "alligators with a ferocious appetite" want is your money. The difference between $50,000 and $25,000 quality cars is mostly in the name. Is the difference worth it? Check out the "replacement cost" of identical parts. Buying a new car? You can paint those $200 stripes for $5 (masking tape, paint brush, paint). Are the oil corporations ripping you off? Their estimated profits will exceed $150 billion for 2008. Ask what their profits were in 2007 and who the major stock holders are.

Our economy is in shambles because of stupidity, greed and ineffective legislation. The first thing our government does is bailout failing businesses. They have done so numerous times in the past and they will continue doing so in the future. Stop. Let the businesses fail. Others will take their place. We may be inconvenient for a while, but the economy will recover without government assistance. What the government needs to do it doesn't do. What it doesn't need to do it does. Frankly, we would be better off if we were to do away with countless laws and regulations. We should ask Congress to take a one year vacation from passing new laws, and instead spend the time getting rid of all the garbage it has spewed out over the years.

Chapter XXII

Federal Budget

S aving the best for the last. Because of dictionary usage, I will refer to it as the Federal Budget. But, we should consider re-naming it the "Annual Bickering Contest." At a specific time of the year Congress, the President, and federal agencies enter into a bickering contest to determine who gets what slice of the pie (budget). The federal budget process is outdated, an antique. Years in and years out, not one government agency knows what funds will be provided, or if they will be provided on a timely basis. It is amazing that we have educated individuals with a BA, MA or PhD who cannot figure out how to budget effectively.

If you buy a house, you budget payments for thirty years. If you buy a car, furniture, appliances or other large items, you budget your payments according to the contract. When Congress approves a long term program or expense, it does not assign a term limit. Therefore, every year they bicker as to the amount to be allotted. That tells agencies to "hold your breath" until we decide the if's, but's or maybe's of the programs. That is about as stupid as you can get. For agencies to plan their future operations effectively and timely they need to know years ahead what to expect in funding. This includes the military.

When Congress approves a program, it needs to establish a re-view process to determine its continuity and/or need to increase or decrease its budget, size and scope. What Congress needs to do is to establish a ten-year budget for agencies at a specific yearly amount, and because of inflation and/or changes in its mission, subject to yearly review. Let me use imaginary amounts. The Department of Education (DOE) needs $10 billion this year, and will need money for the next nine years, exact amount unknown. What Congress should do is to budget $100 billion at $10 billion annually for the next ten years. This tells DOE the how, what and when in planning its operations for a ten-year period. Yearly, the DOE presents to Congress its needs. Congress can than revise that year's DOE budget, and yearly DOE makes adjustments to its programs. But, at least, at the beginning of each year DOE knows, more or less, where it stands financially. That process can be applied to most agencies or departments. While Congress is in its "Annual Bickering Contest," the DOE, and other agencies or departments have funds for continuation of their operations, without interruptions. Congress would have no need for its annual ritual of approving "continuance of operations" resolutions for departments or agencies pending approval of that year's budget. Simple!

The 20-year USA Marshall Plan (USAMP) should be budgeted differently. A review should be made of all materialistic needs (bridges, highways, tunnels, dams, levees, etc.) at current day cost. To this cost would be added an annual inflation rate of 3% to determine total future cost. The USAMP budget could then be established for annual operations, with no further action required from Congress other than for unexpected additional cost due to disasters. If the total cost is determined to be $1.5 trillion, then the initial budget should be established, and the annual budgets increased by 3%. Let us say that the initial budget is $50 billion (this amount is for illustration only). The second year budget would then be $51.5 billion. The third year $53.045 billion, and every year thereafter 3% added to the previous year's cost. This process allows Congress to function more effectively and satisfies the concerns of the taxpayers for they now know that action is being taken to address their current and future needs insofar as the infrastructure is concerned.

Congress should be concerned with the need to effectively address our social needs. Futuristic budgeting can be extremely helpful to Congress. It significantly reduces the time spent on budgeting, thus allowing time to spend on reviewing GAO audits on agencies and organizations which may need to be eliminated or reduced in mission scope, and other urgent matters. To budget social programs under similar arrangements as the USAMP will go a long way toward easing taxpayers' concerns as to their future. It also provides Congress time and opportunity to scrutinize the scope and need of all social programs, with the possibility of centralizing some of those programs under one directorship. If within a given year Congress determines that a particular program is no longer required, then it informs the department or agency that the program will be discontinued at the end of the budget year, and adjusts their future budget.

The most important aspect of futuristic budgeting is that it provides us an excellent insight as to our future needs, cost and tax revenue, and brings peace of mind to Americans as concerns their individual need to plan for their future, and that of their children. Not knowing what to expect year to year from a bickering Congress has become an obstacle to our economy and hinders agencies, businesses and an individual's ability to make long term decisions.

I admit that my futuristic budgeting plan is not perfect. But, anything, anything is better than the annual bickering budget process that Congress imposes on us. The major opposition that Congress can have against futuristic budgeting is that it will hinder political pork barrel spending and easily identify special interest and lobbyist's insertions.

OVERVIEW

H opefully, you will be able to understand my reasoning for a USA MARSHALL PLAN. The plan will bring effective long term economic benefits to all nationwide. I calculate that such a plan will create millions of jobs, lift millions out of poverty, restore financial security to the middle income, create tax revenue in excess of cost, restore our military might, improve our local law enforcement, educate our people, create a skill work force, import an unskilled "guest" work force, reduce and/or eliminate illegal immigration, secure our Medicare and social security programs, provide housing for our poor, rebuild our infrastructure, correct most of our social inadequacies and improve our economic prosperity for decades to come. It can and it will. My intent here is to provide a guideline as to what we need to do and how to do it. So, what can we really do to initiate such a Marshall Plan? I will begin with what I am familiar with.

But, before I do that, consider this. A church pastor gave a 10-year-old boy $100 and told him to do something good that would help somebody. The boy set his mind on doing something. He bought stamps, envelopes and paper, and wrote letters to friends and relatives asking for money to build a house for a poor family. Donations were received and the house built. If a child can do what he did for one family, how much can we adults do for our country, if we set our minds on doing something?

In San Antonio, Texas there is a neighborhood organization, the Avenida Guadalupe Association (AGA). Detailed accomplishments can be found on its website. In general, it has constructed three senior citizen housing complexes, an office building, business incubator, community center, low income housing, and a plaza. It created a housing assistance program, assisted in relocating a pharmacy and an English language teaching facility to the neighborhood, and assisted in obtaining funding to revitalizing a theater into a hub of Hispanic arts and culture. It sponsors the only USA internationally viewed parade celebrating Mexico's independence and an annual fund-raising GALA event. Others have had a positive impact. A 153,000 square feet medical complex and an Olympic size swimming pool were constructed, the high school rebuilt and businesses have begun moving into the area. Another organization, COPS, is responsible for construction of a significant number of new housing in the area and repairs to the infrastructure. Currently, the AGA has a business master plan for a portion of the targeted area. The plan is to construct a professional and business complex, parking garage, a small park, and to improve the plaza. To redevelop the entire business corridor and repopulate the neighborhood will cost approximately $100,000,000, much of which will be recycled and used on other needed projects. How can a Marshall Plan help it and hundreds of other similar associations?

A reasonable grant by the federal government is a good beginning. Grants by the city, state and foundations would help. Donations by billionaires and millionaires could seal an effective beginning. The AGA knows what it is doing. The city is responsible for funding administrative cost. Visit the AGA site and see for yourselves what this effective association is doing and can do. If hundreds of neighborhood associations nationwide were doing what the AGA has done and is doing, our national economy would expand.

Do the math. Should all the funding entities I mentioned join forces and establish a national long term Marshall Plan, effective economic expansion will follow. Billionaires, millionaires and foundations will recoup their donations because their stock market portfolio value will more than double. City, state and federal tax revenue will soar. Businesses will profit. Employment will increase and welfare decrease. I am being realistic. There is no doubt in my mind that within five years the Dow will exceed 15,000; Nasdaq 5,000; S & P 3,000 and the 10-year bond yield 5.0. Consider the slogan of the wealthy, "it takes money to make money." Well, generosity not only makes money, it also generates good will, personal satisfaction and brings peace of mind and tranquility to the life of donors.

The people of Bexar County, Texas, may not know it, but they have a local Marshall Plan in the works. And it is producing results. Bexar County passed a $400 million plus Venue Tax to construct and improve sports facilities and expand tourism opportunities. San Antonio passed a $500 million plus Bond Issue to construct and/or repair our infrastructure and other necessities. School districts passed Bond Issues to construct and improve our educational facilities. Major businesses are constructing facilities. A new four year university will soon be constructed. Organizations and educational and medical institutions have received donations and grants for their missions. While the nation is experiencing an economic downward spiral, Bexar County and the surrounding areas are booming. What we need is for cities nationwide, small and large to adopt some, if not all, of these processes. The economic impact would be astronomical. In San Antonio and the surrounding area, the state is improving and/or reconstructing our interstate highways. We are constantly bombarded with painful and inconvenient, yet necessary, detours and delays. Don't wait on our inept Congress to address your needs.

Other than wasting tax dollars, I have yet to discover what the federal government is doing nationwide to effectively help our economic situation. The idea behind the current $150 billion tax rebate had to be conjured by an educated ignoramus. Like most of you, my share is in the bank earning interest. It could have been used to create a million jobs by repairing our highways, tunnels, dams, bridges, levees, other structures, and cleaning our polluted streams, rivers and lakes. Some of it could have been used to construct three to six salt water desalination plants and plant several million trees. Lord knows we could have used one million new low income housing units. If we cannot get effective legislation and responsible budgeting out of Congress, then it's time to replace those elected officials. Is it time for dissatisfied democrats, republicans and independents to join forces and form a moderate party that will address our needs? Taxpayers need to pledge to themselves to remove ineptness from political office. I do not enjoy criticizing anyone. But, Congress is like a computer; garbage in garbage out.

There are immediate actions that can be taken. At the local level, cities need to schedule a bond issue vote for the purpose of obtaining funds to repair and/or improve their infrastructure. This should include poor neighborhood revitalization and their repopulation. They also need to establish a ten-hour workday four day workweek. Consideration must also be given to resurrecting the use of trolleys as a means of inner city transportation. Counties should schedule a Venue Tax to repair and/or improve their infrastructure, construct recreation centers and parks, and establish a ten-hour workday four day workweek. States need to budget for improvements to state parks and to their highway system. The states also need to establish government offices in poor neighborhoods in order to accelerate business redevelopment in those areas, and to establish a ten-hour workday four day workweek.

The President can take immediate actions. The first one is to establish a ten-hour workday four day workweek for federal agencies. He needs to establish a 60-day term committee to investigate the potential for a cross country high speed passenger railroad system. A 60-day term committee should also be established to determine the potential for salt water desalination plants. He also needs to have two of his Congressional friends submit a bill in the House and Senate to establish a cut off date of the present personal income tax system and a start date of a fair system. The President must establish a process for submission of a long term USA Marshall Plan for nationwide infrastructure repairs and improvements. We, the people, are the ones responsible, and we need to start exercising our responsibilities in order to have Congress take action on our social programs and problems. Don't wait on your neighbors. Instead, bring them along.

What I am asking from people, cities, counties, states and the President are the planning of actions. The planning is not expensive. It is the doing of all asked for that will cost. A long term accomplishment process will allow us to do it. All taxing entities need to study everything mentioned in this book and determine what needs they should take immediate action on. The needs that result in creating jobs must be given priority. For all government-funded work, the President must require that: (1) all material, equipment and supplies be USA made. If they are not, then the SBA must be directed to create a business that will manufacture that required. (2) All businesses awarded contracts must employ only USA citizens. Any business employing illegal immigrants must be disqualified. The contract must be cancelled for any business hiring illegal immigrants after the contract is awarded.

Some final words. Stop using corn and soy bean as a source for alternative fuels. Sugar cane has been proven time and time again to be less costly as an alternative fuel and produces seven times more energy. If you marry sugar cane production with my SWDP concept, we significantly reduce our dependency on foreign oil. While we have a few Congressmen, such as Charlie Gonzalez, who serve with honesty, dignity, integrity and respect, I have no respect for Congress as a whole. Congress, please kill the alligator and retrieve your brains from the swamp.

AS I SAID IN THE BEGINNING, THE FUTURE OF AMERICA IS IN THE HANDS OF ITS PEOPLE. THAT'S YOU. GOD BLESS MY AMERICA. CONGRESS MUST EARN MY RESPECT.

PART II: REVITALIZATION

PART II: REVITALIZATION

Chapter I

United States of America Today

D rive across the USA from the East Coast to the West Coast and from the Mexican Border to the Canadian Border. Sing "America the Beautiful." From the highways we can see rolling prairies, mountains, deer, rabbits, birds, squirrels, ducks, geese and the panoramic countryside. Winter time we go to ski resorts, warmer states or spend time by the fireplace. Summer time we cannot resist playing sports or attend sporting events, going to sunny beaches, swimming pools, on picnics or tour national parks. We spend time walking in the park, visiting the zoo, taking in a movie, going out dancing, visiting friends and spending time with our children and their activities.

Daily, new businesses are born, expand or fail. People are hired or fired. We wake up not knowing if we still have our jobs. Some of us, through social security, 401k, IRAs, or a combination of plans succeed in savings for retirement. The poor have no choice but to rely on small social security checks. The economy expands or retracts. The stock market goes up and down. Whether the economy is up or down we spend billions on clothing, appliances, furniture, real estate, vehicles, diet pills, cosmetics, entertainment, recreation, exercise equipment, medicine, rent, mortgage payments, utilities and food. We have a good life. Nothing is impossible in the USA.

That is, until you drive on city streets that most people never see or fear to drive on. Third world conditions do exist in America. Have you driven through those neighborhoods where you find dilapidated housing, business corridors with vacant lots and buildings, overgrown weeds, bar after bar and condemnable structures. Many streets reveal the encroachment of the creeping urban blight. In the meantime, city governments find money to build professional sport stadiums, beautify parks, and grant businesses property and business tax abatements, create special taxing districts and postpone their annexation. What our city governments refuse to understand is that continuing to ignore people's needs and their refusal to revitalize poor neighborhoods are detrimental to the city and the poor people's efforts to escape from poverty.

Blighted neighborhoods, where businesses and jobs have disappeared and the remaining jobs pay minimum wages, are the breeding grounds for failure, expansion of poverty and creation of criminals. We need to start at the bottom by providing the poor with a stable and secured home environment (foundation) before we build the roof (education). Revitalization of the inner city, especially the poor neighborhoods, must be given priority equal to that of education and jobs.

Chapter II

Cost

G overnments, corporations, businesses, foundations and people in general are afraid that it will cost a trillion dollars to revitalize America's inner cities. Maybe it will. But the consequences of not doing anything carries a higher cost in money and life. One out of every one hundred Americans is in jail or on probation. Over the years they have cost the taxpayers trillions of dollars. Add to that the trillions we have spent over the years on welfare and social programs.

Neighborhood Acceleration Revitalization Associations (NARA), by recycling funds in our dilapidating and low income neighborhoods, can construct low income family housing, low income senior citizen housing, community facilities, and small business retail centers, demolish dilapidation and remove criminal breeding grounds. The money is not wasted. The recycling of money will generate economic activity for an extended period. Manufacturing of goods will increase, thousands of jobs and businesses will be created or expanded, disposable income for the poor (and middle income) will increase and welfare rolls decrease. Low income children in affordable and decent shelters are more responsible, better disciplined and usually more successful and less likely to become criminals.

We need to stop the bleeding, in money and in life. The window of opportunity is open for us to revitalize inner cities throughout the USA and create the environment for a long term expanding economy. The cost is minor compared to the significant benefits to be gained by all taxpayers.

Chapter III

Constituting the NNARC and NARA

C ongress needs to establish a National Neighborhood Accelerated Revitalization Center (NNARC) to administer a revitalization program and provide it with the funds needed.
Neighborhood Acceleration Revitalization Associations (NARA)
can and will do a better job than any other agency or organization.

The NNARC and NARA charters and by-laws should be written by the appointees using the contract services of an attorney in
order to proceed with a standard policy and a cohesive manner. The
NNARC should deal directly with the NARA (no federal, state or
city agencies). The USA should be divided into ten districts, each
with an NNARC account manager.

The NNARC will create the NARA where none exists. The
NARA administrative expenses must be paid for by the cities. The
NARA Board of Directors needs to be elected to three (3) year
terms by neighborhood residents and consists of nine (9) non-paid
members. The Board will hire the Director of the Association who,
in turn, will hire the staff.

Chapter IV

Mission Objective

T he mission of the NARA will be to revitalize the poor inner city
neighborhoods. This is to be accomplished by repopulation
through construction of affordable housing and community facilities, and redeveloping of the business sector.

The NARA will render a Master Plan detailing the needs of the
neighborhood with an assessment of the dilapidation, social, economic, educational, physical and environmental conditions present.
The plan will be updated every five (5) years in order to address the
then current situation.

Chapter V

Businesses

There are stretches of business corridors that cannot sustain extensive business development. While some businesses can be grandfathered at their present locations, they and new businesses should be encouraged to locate/relocate to small retail centers constructed at key neighborhood intersections. These centers should house retail and professional businesses, as well as government offices and health clinics. Hazardous material businesses must not be allowed in the neighborhoods. The concept of grouping businesses that feed off of each other should be maximized. Efforts should be made to have investors construct the retail centers, with NARA construction considered only as a last resort. Government entities have numerous programs that should be utilized in assisting businesses wanting to relocate to the area. The NARA will ask local government entities to grant property tax abatements and reduction of business taxes to assist new and expanding businesses in the area.

Chapter VI

Low Income Family Housing

Advocates of the poor want some low income family housing constructed in better neighborhoods. Others want the low income to be able to purchase housing instead of renting. Whether or not there is merit to these concerns should not be allowed to interfere with the revitalization process. The providing of housing by the NARA must be for the purpose of providing affordable shelter, repopulation and revitalization of poor neighborhoods.

The NARA will utilize two programs for housing the poor. One is the Low Income Housing Dual Purchase System (LIHDPS). The other is the Low Income Life Term Housing Lease System (LILTHLS). I will use Texas (a property state) as to how the systems should work.

The NARA constructs or purchases a house for $100,000. Under the LILTHLS it leases that house to the poorest of the poor at the monthly rate of: 1% ($100 base rent) of the construction or purchase cost; $200 property tax; $60 insurance; total $360. The base rent will never increase, but the lease rate will increase when the property tax and the insurance rates increase. The lessee pays for normal property maintenance and repairs not covered by insurance (plugged sinks/toilets, etc.), utilities, telephone, pest control, internet, cable/dish/direct TV or other services desired. When insurance repairs (hail, etc.) are required, the NARA pays the deductible. The lessee must have at least two (2) children under the age of ten (10). The purpose of this requirement is to provide school age children so that schools can be repopulated.

Under the LIHDPS the NARA constructs houses. It then sells the house to low income families. The NARA loans (not grants) the buyer $25,000 down payment assistance. This loan is to be repaid when the buyer dies, vacates or sells the house at its then future value. If the house is inherited, the heirs must repay the loan. If the loan is not repaid, the NARA will foreclose on the house, collect its debt and deposit the balance to the buyer's (deceased) estate. This action prevents the heirs, who may be doctors, nurses, CPA, etc. from inheriting the $25,000 which may be worth some $100,000 at the time of death of the buyer.

If these two systems were in effect in 1950 there would be no need for low income housing today; no low income housing authorities; no government housing agencies; and poor neighborhoods would not be experiencing dilapidation. Today we would be saving billions of dollars. All housing services for the poor would now be handled by a small staffed NARA, and not by 1,000 manned housing authorities. Under the LILTHLS, periodic investigations should be made to determine if the lessee is still qualified to remain in the leased unit.

The concept calls for providing housing for the poor, but not above the minimum required to house a family. Developers should not be used as their involvement adds ten to twenty percent to the construction cost. Construction contracts must be negotiated directly between the NARA and the contractor doing the actual work. The NARA should be the developer.

Both lessee and buyer are to be qualified if they can prove that they are low income. Copies of income tax returns for the previous five years must be submitted. They must also sign a statement authorizing the NARA to verify any information provided on the application and allow for any investigation deemed necessary. Lessee and buyer, and their teenage children, must be required to take a drug test at a facility selected by the NARA, with results provided directly to the NARA. The drug test form must contain spaces for index finger prints. One print will be taken at the NARA office and the other immediately before the drug test. Use of drugs or refusal to take a drug test will result in disqualification. Families with criminal or domestic disturbance records must be disqualified if such actions occurred within the five-year period prior to the date of application. These actions must be taken for two reasons: prevent undesirables from leasing or buying; their use of drugs and behavior will result in nonpayment of rents or mortgages.

The NARA will ask local government taxing entities to grant five property tax abatements in order to make housing more afford-able to the poor at the onset. The abatements should be: 1st year 90%, 2nd 80%, 3rd 70%, 4th 60% and 5th 50%.

Chapter VII

Low Income Senior Citizen Housing

The low income senior citizen housing centers should contain 100 units. Maximum security features and outdoor congregation areas must be provided. The NARA must provide management for the centers. If land is available, 'victory gardens' will be provided to keep seniors busy and reduce facility costs by providing food substances.

My next suggestion will arouse controversy. There are cities that have substantial land available where small senior citizen villages can be built. Seniors should be allowed to live with dignity, integrity and respect, and not allowed to just wither away waiting for the eventuality that old age brings. The villages should provide for victory gardens, some livestock, pets, recreational facilities, a nursing home, businesses that cater to seniors (manned part time by seniors). The villages should be managed by the NARA. Nurses and physician assistants should staff a medical clinic. By keeping seniors busy and having animals and pets around them, they will have fewer medical, physical and mental illnesses. The younger and healthy seniors can work part time doing various jobs, such as janitorial, landscaping, secretarial, caregivers and maintenance.

This concept does not 'farm out' seniors. Instead, it adds quality to their life by giving them purpose, fulfillment, dignity, integrity, respect and worthiness.

Chapter VIII

Community Facilities

C ommunity facilities are essential for creation of a community spirit of togetherness, where they can come together for recreation and enjoyment, restoring pride, dignity, integrity and respect. An indoor community center is a must and should be made available for weddings, birthdays, anniversaries and other needs. The NARA may use it for organizational fund-raising events and for board of director's meetings.

An indoor/outdoor recreational facility is essential. It should contain basketball, tennis and volleyball courts, as well as a game room, swimming pool and other needs. A park where residents can gather should be constructed. Consideration should be given to constructing a combined park and plaza. A low-cost child and adult day care facility may prove valuable. Other community facilities may be constructed as needed.

The NARA must retain ownership of all community facilities and be responsible for their maintenance and management. The main emphasis of community facilities should be to revitalize neighborhoods, make them an integral part of the city and one that contributes not only to the needs of the neighborhood but also to the needs of all city residents. The NARA will have the right of refusing rental to any party deemed undesirable or any party that does not establish control as concerns the sales of prohibited items (especially to children).

Chapter IX

Dilapidation

D ilapidation will prove to be the most difficult undertaking in the revitalization process, especially where property owner-ship requires an extensive search. Where essential properties have condemned structures or where structures have deteriorated, the NARA must negotiate a purchase price. All properties must be inspected and if determined that potential environmental hazards exist, an environmental evaluation must be made and reported to the proper authorities. Such properties will not be purchased until it is certified that the hazards have been removed. Garbage land-filled properties are not to be purchased unless it is feasible cost-wise to recover the land for usage.

Where properties are essential for the construction of commu-nity facilities and the owners prove uncooperative, action to invoke "imminent domain" must be utilized. Structures suitable for condo-minium usage should be given considerable attention. Also, the county, city, state and federal governments may own unoccupied properties that are not producing tax revenue. Efforts should be made to determine the possibility of having such properties donated.

Chapter X

Other Factors

I t must be recognized that government entities have established laws, rules, policies and procedures as concerns some of the actions the revitalization must take. Where such rulings prove to be obstacles, action should be taken to remove or have them modified to meet needs. There may also be instances where rulings have not been established but may need to be established when essential to the revitalization effort. The governing entity must be contacted in order to establish such a ruling.

Buyer, lessee and contractor conversations with NARA personnel must be recorded and made available to parties on a "need to know" basis.

The NARA may receive donations and grants as long as special treatment is not required.

All NARA meetings must be open and public attendance permitted. Executive (closed) meetings are not to be allowed. NARA transparency is essential.

The NNARC shall not make loans or grants to entities other than the NARA.

Chapter XI

Alternative

We should remain aware of past and present programs, such as the New Deal, War on Poverty, Welfare, Aid to Dependent Children and others. Most have been eliminated, modified or reduced in funding. Congress may be reluctant to establish a revitalization program. We must then look for funding by city, county and state governments, and from foundations and wealthy individuals.

Cities should pass a "pay as you go" revitalization sales tax. Cities may want to pass a bond issue. Whatever method is used, we must look at revitalization as a program where "failure is not an option."

Do not forget that our forefathers made America what it was in the past, and we make the America of today and tomorrow. In the end, it is ours and our children and grandchildren's future that should be our main concern.

Chapter XII

Program Benefits

A s the buyer and lessee make their payments, we recycle (roll over) the funds. The money they spend buying furniture, appliances, dishware, tools, equipment, and home accessories also recycles. The spending of money under the revitalization effort will generate prolonged economic activity and have a positive impact on the stock market. The poor and middle income prosper because a prolonged economic expansion creates long term job security, pay raises, interest, income, and more flexibility in their financial and economic activities.

It is true that the more disposable income the wealthy has the more they invest (trickle down), thus creating opportunities for the low and middle income. Still, the more disposable income the low and middle income has the more money trickles up to the wealthy. Low income families benefit because they now have affordable housing. Businesses will prosper because billions will be spent on construction materials, supplies, tools and equipment. Consumers will have more disposable income to spend on retail needs.

You may select any category of society and social issues you want. One thing remains clear. The revitalization effort will have a positive impact and benefit all people nationwide.

Conclusion

It may be difficult to imagine Congress establishing a revitalization program. But it will if enough people get behind the effort and exert the necessary pressure on their elected officials. What we get out of it: prolonged economic growth; thousands, if not millions, of new jobs; new businesses; old businesses expand; dilapidation is eliminated; tax entities get new tax revenue; urban blight disappears, affordable low income housing is provided; the environment that creates criminals, deters one from studying, and causes poverty to expand, is substantially reduced. Job security is assured for millions. It may be difficult for anyone to believe that revitalization will do as much as is claimed. But, it can, and will revitalize America while creating priceless prosperity nationwide. The best way to help ourselves and the world is by first effectively helping ourselves.

Short and long term, the benefits resulting from the revitalization of the United States of America far outweigh the cost, for it benefits our people and our nation. An individual with foresight can visualize the significant impact of revitalizing some 1,000 neighborhoods, over a period of time, across the country.

Because we have not effectively aided low and middle income families in the past and our governments have ignored our inner city neighborhoods, we now have millions of criminals, a high rate of crime, urban blight and deterioration in America. Just imagine the savings in money and grief if we act to prevent one million individuals from becoming criminals and reduce the high school and college drop-out rates. We can do it.

In the end, our Will, Spirit, Historical Courage and Fortitude will determine the results. We have reached that point in time when we have the Means and Reasons to take action, and where, as I have stated before, "failure cannot be an option."

PART III: Neighborhood Revitalization

The Avenida Guadalupe Association
San Antonio, Texas

PART III: NEIGHBORHOOD REVITALIZATION

Avenida Guadalupe Association

I n March of 1979, Father Edmundo Rodriquez, priest at Our Lady of Guadalupe Catholic Church in San Antonio, Texas gathered his flock. For hours we discussed the situation of the Westside of San Antonio, Texas (City Council District 5). We finally agreed on what the problems were and what needed to be done to revitalize the area, and to meet again. In October of 1979 Father Rodriquez again gathered his flock. This time the Avenida Guadalupe Association (AGA) was created and the Board of Directors elected. The first action taken by the Board was to contract for a study of all aspects of the target area and the creation of a Master Plan. The study confirmed our findings discussed in March of 1979. The findings were:

Poorest Congressional District in the USA (1979).
Extensive house and business structure dilapidation.
Weeds and garbage on vacant properties.
Aging population-area depopulation.
High unemployment-low income-few jobs.
Few businesses- too many unsavory businesses.
High crime rate.
High rate of teenage delinquency.
High rate of high school absentee.
High drop out rate from high school.
High rate of teenage pregnancy.

Absentee landlords-high rate of vacancies.
No recreational facilities-homelessness.
Extremely poor infrastructure.
Ignored by the city, state and federal governments.

The mission of the AGA became clear. To revitalize the area and directly address the problems we needed to: repopulate the neighborhood; redevelop the business corridor; create job and business opportunities; demolish dilapidation; remove unsavory businesses; eliminate the criminal breeding environment; and construct low income single family and senior citizen housing, community facilities, business offices and small retail centers. We accepted the difficulties that would be confronted.

In 1980 the first revitalization efforts were launched. We supported our sister organization, the Guadalupe Cultural and Arts Center, in obtaining funds to renovate the Guadalupe Theater which is now the hub in the USA of Mexican and Mexican America arts, crafts, dance, literature and culture. Simultaneously, funds were obtained for the AGA to purchase and clear (demolish dilapidation and remove unsavory businesses) one city block for construction of the Guadalupe Plaza (visited by the Pope in 1987). Between 1982 and 1990, while assisting a pharmacy/clinic to relocate adjacent to the plaza, funds were obtained to purchase and clear a one-half city block for construction of a business incubator mini-mall. Then funds dried up. We also initiated the 16th of September Mexican Parade to celebrate Mexico's Independence (televised internationally). Every September, the AGA holds an annual GALA event to raise funds and honor individuals and businesses that support the AGA effort.

In the mid 1990s the funding drought ended. Since then, funds have been granted to construct three low income senior citizen centers, a learning center, children's playground, renovate the old Progresso Theater into a community center, construct several houses and purchase some properties. While the AGA has been revitalizing the area, other organizations and businesses have joined the effort. The High School has been rebuilt, indoor Olympic size swimming pool constructed, several restaurants have opened, and an old store was renovated into a crafts district. Finally, a 153,000 square foot medical facility, the University Center for Community Health/Texas Diabetes Institute and Research Center, was constructed.

The AGA initiated a Housing Counseling Program which was approved by the Department of Housing and Urban Development and by the Texas Department of Housing and Community Affairs. The AGA partnered in 2006 with the San Antonio Neighborhood Commercial Revitalization Program. The purpose of the program is to help poor neighborhoods throughout the city promote and market their business districts, preserve unique physical assets, plan private and public improvements, promote business retention and recapture the economic vitality of the neighborhoods.

The most pressing needs, to construct sufficient low income houses, repopulate the area, construct a recreation center and retail center, demolish more dilapidated structures, locate more businesses to the area and create substantial well-paying jobs, have eluded the AGA. There are other needs: plant trees, install more lights, another playground, sidewalks, parking lot, child day care center, amphitheater, jogging trails, purchase and repair vacant houses, install lights on the bridge, install additional lights in the neighborhood, and have the city control animals. The reality is that few funds are presently being granted to the AGA. Please, view www.agatx.org and read what the AGA is all about. You are welcome to tour the neighborhood and visit during business hours. (1–210–223–3151) (FAX 1–210–223–4405).

ABOUT THE AUTHOR

I was born in the poor Westside neighborhood of San Antonio, Texas, Hispanic and Catholic. I am supposed to be a Democrat, but am an Independent. My views differ from most of my peers because of my upbringing by a stern mother, having served in the military for twenty-six years, lived in various locales nationwide and overseas and met people of all races, religions, color, nationalities and social standings. While many of my peers have lived their life inside the box, I have not. I am a graduate of the School of Aerospace Medicine Division "Industrial Hygiene Measurement Course" and have three years of college, having majored in Accounting. The only notable thing I have done in my life is being the 1979 co-founder and first president of the Avenida Guadalupe Association in San Antonio, Texas.

My views are a combination of moderate liberalism and moderate conservatism. However, after eight years of misguided conservatism we need some liberalism. When it comes to America, my beliefs are simple. If enough Americans gather to correct a wrong, whether it is materialistic or social, it will be corrected. Thanks to our forefathers, we are the luckiest people in the world. There is no one like us in the world. I am a proud American.

I have four beliefs that I want to share with you. "When you dwell in the past, you have no future." "When God walks with you, you achieve." "When you walk with God, we all achieve." "For many, money is their God. Make sure your's isn't."

Eugenio Macias

LaVergne, TN USA
03 November 2010

203354LV00010B/40/P